Nature 123

DISCOVERY BOOKS

ISBN: 1-55013-250-4

Discovery Books
The International Division of
Key Porter Books Limited
70 The Esplanade,
Toronto, Ontario,
Canada   M5E 1R2

Printed and bound in Hong Kong

1

One koala

2

Two raccoons

3

Three bears

4

Four elephants

5

Five zebras

6

Six wolves

7

Seven puffins

8

Eight camels

9
Nine deer

10

Ten rams

11
Eleven fish

12

Twelve ducks

13

Thirteen
bighorn sheep

14

Fourteen swans

15

Fifteen
Canada geese

Nature Notes

One koala
Koalas are found only in Australia. They are tree-dwellers and spend almost all their time in eucalyptus trees.
(Photo: Wayne Lynch)

Two raccoons
Raccoons often make their den in the hollows of trees and generally have three or four baby raccoons in a litter.
(Photo: Julie Habel, First Light)

Three bears
Brown bear cubs stay with their mother for up to three years. They learn to survive on their own by watching and imitating their mothers.
(Photo: Wayne Lynch)

Four elephants
African elephants are the largest land mammals. They feed on a wide variety of vegetation including grasses, shrubs and leaves from trees.
(Photo: Brian Beck)

Five zebras
Zebras are found in Africa and mainly eat grass. They sleep standing — only young foals lie down.
(Photo: J.D. Taylor)

Six wolves
Wolves live in packs made up of a mother and father, an uncle or maybe an aunt and some young wolf cubs.
(Photo: Peter McLeod, First Light)

Seven puffins
Common puffins are found along the Atlantic coast of North America from Greenland to Maine. Puffins are excellent underwater swimmers.
(Photo: Wayne Lynch)

Eight camels
Camels have adapted well to their desert home — their ears are small and hairy and their eylashes are long to keep out the sand.
(Photo: Guido Alberto Rossi, The Image Bank)

Nine deer
Deer are found in parts of Europe, Asia and North America. There are many different species of deer. The deer in this photo are Père David's deer and they are originally from China.
(Photo: Thomas Kitchin, First Light)

Ten rams
The rams in this photo are male Dall's Sheep. They feed on the slopes of mountains in western North America, and climb to great altitudes.
(Photo: Karl Sommerer)

Eleven fish
The school of fish in this picture is swimming in a shoal off the Grand Cayman Islands in the Caribbean.
(Photo: Rubens Neves da Rocha Fihlo, The Image Bank)

Twelve ducks
Mallards are the most common and widely distributed of all ducks. It is usual for the female to lay ten or more eggs.
(Photo: Rolf Kraiker)

Thirteen bighorn sheep
These sheep can scale a mountain slope at up to fifteen miles per hour. The female's horns are thin and spiky; the male's curve, sometimes forming a full circle.
(Photo: Brian Milne, First Light)

Fourteen swans
These are tundra swans, found in northern North America and Siberia. They have straight necks, unlike mute swans whose necks form an S-shape.
(Photo: Karl Sommerer)

Fifteen Canada geese
With their long black necks and white chinstraps, Canada geese are easy to recognize. There are at least twelve types of Canada goose. The giant Canada goose can weigh more than 20 pounds.
(Photo: Rolf Kraiker)